Praise for

The Ego Rhythm

This powerful collection pulses with the beat of the human heart, capturing love, identity, and existential reflection. It offers the resonant harmony of an orchestra tuning to the concertmaster's, exploring the depths of youthful rebellion, disillusionment, and complex relationships. The storytelling is beautifully direct, illustrating an emotional knot trapped within a man's throat before the animalistic bellow roars, mirroring the chaos of modern life and philosophical musings on existence. *The Ego Rhythm* is an endorsement of life's intricate dance, a compelling invitation to embrace the chaotic beauty of being.

—**Victoria Lopez**, McAllen Poet Laureate 2022 & 2025

Kenan Phillip's *The Ego Rhythm* explores what it means to be alive in the 21st century, informed by the past and the present, yearning for more and in awe at the same time amidst "the insistence / of existence." The work comes of age as it grapples with the meanings of desire, suffering, death, and life. And more, if that is possible. It sings the blues as it uplifts, reminding us that to seek deeper meaning in our lives can be a bittersweet and affirming process.

—**Emmy Pérez**, Texas Poet Laureate 2020

The Ego Rhythm

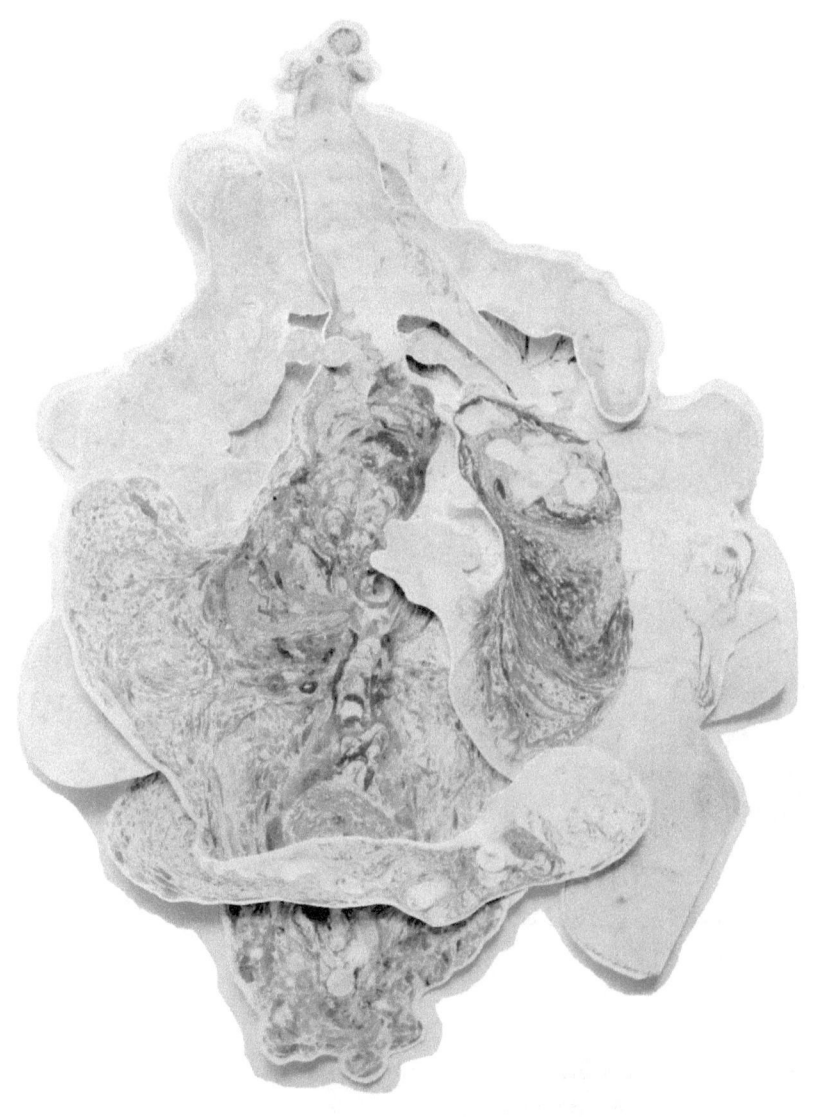

poetry by

Kenan Wilson Phillip

FLOWERSONG
PRESS

The Ego Rhythm

FLOWERSONG
P R E S S

poetry by
Kenan Wilson Phillip

table of contents

I. THE BARYONIC PARABLE

II. AN ELEGY FOR THE STILL LIVING

The Ego Rhythm

I.

THE BARYONIC PARABLE

bar·y·on·ic
adjective
of or referring to the fundamental physical particles called baryons, or anything which is composed of them, such as neutrons, protons, and atoms.

the majority of visible matter in the universe is baryonic.

par·a·ble
noun
a simple story used to illustrate a moral or spiritual lesson.

snakeskin and stucco, scorpions and sin, white haciendas towering over still lakes, smoke misting the air on a winter morning, old shoes dyed grey with dust from all the places you've never been

a breath sucked in for a thousand years and let out very suddenly all at once a deluge thundering over the Rockies to pull down the conqueror's temples all set to the snarl-backed blues rhythm that believe you me is beating hypnotically at the end of time

music is sex is fire is story is language is a math is love is a tongue (a tongue) a tongue a tongue spitting dreams and lies and white little furies in all our minds so close your eyes and listen

lazy days and lazy years, still summers under a cooling sun in the shadow of chirping cypresses, feet tapping endlessly to the melody of guitar strings. coal-black black-blue streets like cogs in a metal machine, and steam rising in unholy clouds from the tar that cooks beneath,

and over it all that same bouncy jazzy groovy rhythm snarling into eternity, ten parts the funk and ten parts the Revelation, something like an orgasmic grunt, or a sin-soaked parable from the lips of the late Lord Byron

and it sounds just a little bit like this:

lies

My mama was a liar
(no she wasn't)
and so I am too
(yes I am)
I learned it like I learned the samba
(I can't dance):
slowly and bitterly,
with little love lost for my teacher

Afterwards,
I learned to kiss like I learned to lie:
with lots of tongue and lots of heart,
as easily as breathing, and
with about as much meaning

My lies have taught themselves how to hang
low and heavy on the vine,
and they have stretched out and grown,
crisscrossing this nation end to end:
black scars
or railroad lines

I'll have you know, then,
I built that all myself
lie lying on lie,
uncounted millions of them,
lie lying on lie —

spite spitting spite
And you know what else?
I loved it,
Every single second
(no I didn't)

the song from the city

this, here
is the song from the city.

the city
where your
fingertips are
iced over with
the iron ideal,
where
the rum
moves
like hot silk
in your throat,

where the cats
are all twisting
like
worms
on the
boulevards,
shaking off
their
silver
skins
under the
silver moon,
because they,
too, understand

that if you have to die,
die to music.

john henry

they say John Henry drove nails through the mountains
until his heart burst,
but old John Henry and his sparking hammer
couldn't hold a candle
to all the things I've hammered down
into myself

and I'd bet he doesn't have shit on you, either

How many years do you think it would take you to pull up all the
railways in this country with your bare hands?

form

if the subject demands
a certain disorder
don't twist your head off
or the formalists win.
five

klan kid

I saw a lion cub
tanning in the sun
cute as cute could be
and wondered when
he would learn to kill. He had
bright golden fur
like a sunray
and eyes like the odd blue sky.
He was as cute as cute could be
yet all I could wonder
was when he'd learn to kill —
or if he already knew?

whalefall

outside my window
there are teflon angels rioting on the bannisters
mothers laughing in the morgues
palm trees standing at attention on colonel row
dog eat dog ear
whalefall (good eats).

all alone in the dark,
the jewel squid searches for a mate.

a diagram of the solar system

Bodies whirling out
in the
darkness,
a gravitational gyro:
wheels in wheels
in wheels (in worlds).
Around and around they go,
blindly fluttering in flesh,
a cosmic conga line —
and every one
feeling
blindly at a hole
in their tongue
where a language
should have been.

flow lightning

no time, no pace, no breath, no heat,
no place,
rainwater pooling in your boots, shivering,
but still —

a snowstorm in the sockets of her skull,
flickering, cold,
the wide world white in the whites of her eyes,
but still —

and it knocks you off balance
again,
the sheer intensity of being living, a living being
but still —

so low and deep in your guts, the
violence of it,
(you really *can* teach an animal to hate)
but still —

the night stretches thin
between midnight and morning,
a black bridge with no railings
but still —

the stooped shape of a mountain
hidden behind the clouds,
which has somehow caught you by surprise
but still —

you can tell by the twisted
curve of her feet (like a bow, almost)
that she used to dance
but still —

but still
open your mouth
flow lightning

reconstructive hedonism

The gurus, they said meditate,
the priests said to pray
the screens said — "Worship!"
the man said
well, you know
what the man said.

For a happy change of pace, dip your brain in nicotine and iodine
and THC and MDMA and Japanese rice wine and formaldehyde and
whatever else is in that unholy chemical blend that's driving those
genius madmen ranting and raving about the meaning of life outside
of a Costco at 3:30 AM on a Tuesday night, vomiting galaxies like
pearls as they go (pressed like coal into brilliance by their battered
livers), leaving something that everybody else has always wanted
swirling in the gutters.

midyear

That familiar scent which is as weird and wonderful as the happy incident of your own birth, and is at other times capable of reminding you, if only faintly, of oranges. Can you hear it beating under your toes? There are the wondrous patterns woven backwards and forwards in both sinew and satin, there are tea parties held sincerely and without the least irony on Golgotha Hill, there are ancient and indistinct faces burned into the sides of the pyramids, and there is each breath fluttering in an iron cage, not unlike a witch's wind moving terrible and certain under heaven.

Through it all there is your heart moving like a thresher, an endless cutting force always expanding, expending, exhausting. This must be the nail they spoke of, which runs straight up through the foot of god.

the gita

pound your body like an old kettle drum
without rhythm or mercy

and listen to the soft sounds it makes
right before it breaks

this is that sound
or something like it

too hot

it is too hot, these days,
and the bugs are dying
and the world is getting warmer and
people are growing
colder,
and the bugs are all dying.

it is too hot,
and everywhere you look,
there are indescribable and innumerable
little horrors. All over the place,
more and more, things
are simply
broken, or maybe were never right at all.

it is too hot,
and we are growing shrill,
shrill and desperate and ugly,
and more than ever
we are staggeringly
utterly,
finally,
alone.

it is too hot,
and the planes are passing overhead,
packed to the brim with people like cattle in cans,
all of whom are dreaming strange and ludicrous

things, and it seems that everything
is out of proportion,
blown up
like a tick on a slide under a microscope,
except it is not a tick, it is the world,
but like the tick
it is wriggling.

it is too hot,
and all the bugs are dying,
and nothing anywhere
feels as if it has been right
for a very long time,

and somewhere in the middle of it all
I must love you,
still.

hair of the dog

when the act of living stops and you have to live again,
when your mistakes are laid out all in a row in the cold light of day,
what then?

don't worry, I've got a cure for you
100% foolproof
guaranteed effective, or your money back:

think
(just for a minute)
about drugs and war
and sex and god
and fast-food empires

and how the faith of the slaves
became the faith of the kings

about electrons and energy
bar codes and blood diamonds
hybrid cars and high rises
angel dust and porn stars

think
(just for a minute)

on atoms with broken nuclei —
disconnected
like fractures of a fracture

or a vision of a future:
digital clones dancing in the dark
to a terabyte waltz conducted by billionaires

think
(just for a minute)

on silicone sirens wailing from the streets,
on dust devils and single mothers
with more pride than sense
struggling to make ends meet

on bible mantras and hypocrisy
on sodomy and rhapsody (and isolation too)

on dreams and ghunas and the illiquid price of your own self-hatred
on all the blooming things that never were

think
(just for a minute)

on the systems that broke us
(the ones that we built)
and sold you yourself
(or a self)
for just $79.99
(taxes not included)
think
about fear and fire and the taste of hot lips
about what we have and what we've lost
about the maybes and the babies
and all the truths that you feel but can't touch

and all the starving artists
hunched over in the predawn darkness
sucking down poison clouds with ritualistic passion
banishing their devils with the coming of the sun.

think on all that
and on the rising oceans of the always-tomorrow
(here today)
and all the years we deserved to have
and all the things we should have been
(and never were, but might be if we could only remember how)

think
on how our times are like a deep breath — sucked in very suddenly,
held for a thousand years,
and now let out
all at once

gnaw on all that for a minute or two
and trust me,
your hangover will clear right up.

nothing quite like the hair of the dog that bit you

the men

do not trust men who yearn to be boys again —
they have no sense of perspective,
and no real rules,
and no love for anything which matters
and they would sooner
eat you whole,
little Wendy,
than leave never-never land

do not trust men who say they killed the boys they were
        not because they tried
but because they must have failed:
they've performed a procedure which didn't stick,
and the ugly thing which lived
        has yet to forgive itself

do not trust men who are still boys —
        innocence moves
        glinting
        behind their eyes, bright
        like an angler fish;
underneath all that baby fat,
they have grown too lean
        and too hungry

most of all, do not trust men who say
they *do not* yearn to be boys again,
because they are lying.

superego

And you straighten your shoulders with a new seriousness,
suddenly too aware of your skin,
of the tightness of your face
sitting on your flesh,
of the hours
moving rapidly over your bones.

A new uncertainty settles: you are not living right,
you are not correctly human,
you are perhaps
a great and tremendous nothing.

Behind,
rising just as quickly;
a new hope,
a little lie:
there is, of course, still time.

perspectives on a bullfight

somewhere there's a brass organ wailing at the bottom of the stairs

and there's a cat in the alley that's
stuck in the rain, howling his heart out to hell

and there's old Billie Holiday, her eyes streaked with
tears, singing her heart out into the smoke; and there's

the bullfighter, long and brown,
with his
oiled mustache and his
bright silk leggings,
moving as he has moved a hundred
and one times before. And this matador,
this
man of murder,
he is hiding the skinny length of himself
behind the whirlpool swirling of his cape,
which is dragging up the dust
into billowing clouds of gold.

the bull has been cut already,
six times, and the cuts are
deep. It is dying,
and it knows it is dying,
but still, it is a bull,

so it will die bloody,
and give a good show

(because,
well,
wouldn't you?)

the beast and the bullfighter
dance in the dirt,
their sharp   points   rising

and somewhere Billie Holiday croons into a smoke-filled room

and the man moves
as he has moved a hundred and one times,

but on the hundred-and-second time,
perhaps he does not want it as badly
as he has wanted it
all of the many times before

a shadow splits the sand

(or perhaps,
crosses the sun,
like a wink)

and he moves only a
hair too slow --
a
fraction, really,
a narrow second.

even the bull is surprised
to find his horns
dripping red.
he snorts his disbelief
into a corpse.

And the sound the man makes
right before he dies
reminds me of Billie,
long and slender
and still so young,
clearing her throat into the mic
and starting to sing.

the art of taking it in stride

ice like the world on your tongue
and the world like a nail right through you
it's 5 o'clock somewhere
and I'm lying with a smile
but you have to
take these things in stride, you know?

which things?

oh,
you know:
the darkness under the moving wheel
the slow silence between breaths
and the hammering sound of a heart
like a drum when the drummer has lost the beat

but that's the little stuff,
you get a handle on it pretty quick,
usually, but
if you want to get serious about it —

there is life, like a net thrown wide
and there are wet things on hot streets, breathing to the beat,
and there is the still shape of your father in the distance
before you ever even learned he was human,
or the pop of sugar sharp on your tongue,
or the bedroom stink of skin on skin,
or the mammoth bellow of a train moving icily in the night,

or the terrible shine of metal in a mirror, angled just right,
and there is the whole of this stolen land,
still alive anyway, more alive, now,

and there is the hand of a lover open wide like a bird's talons in the
dark,
and the godlike hugeness of a man when his name is too thin,
and there is all the splendid crap of earth,
the stuff you drink in anyway

and under everything,
under all of it,
there's a bend,
like the low arc of heaven,

a bend
and a break

fire and rod

sprint to the edge
cut along the line
drive through the weeds
spit through the spin, and
you might
feel yourself   turning
with the strikers

feel your whole

body

move
by the fire and rod

feel
how slow it is, how red it is,
how it quakes, how it churns,
how it pulls in to the edges,
how it bends softly at the break,
how it vents
the vilest things
and keeps on going on.

deferred

Can you hear it?
Simmering, rumbling, rising up?
There's a familiar roar going round,
there's something old boiling high,
hissing like a kettle in the dead of night.
Everybody (but everybody) knows
That something just ain't right.

Well baby, can you hear it,
The boogie-woogie rumble?
Oh baby, have you heard
The funky old word?
And baby, have you felt
The spine-tingling beat?

Grumbling stomachs and hungry hearts, eyes blinking to a new day,
the narcissistic rumblings of a generation doomed before their birth,
the acrid thick smell wafting on the wind over the breaking tides, a
breath sucked in and held for ten thousand years until your lungs are
just about fit to burst, an animal scream echoing out over the radio
waves, a simulacrum of a self constructed from bits and bytes and
maybe numbers, a dream yoked to the earth and nailed to the dirt,
serenaded by the gut deep grunting of lovers lost in time and in each
other, impossibly and blissfully high on the last dregs of whatever their
parents could leave behind, shedding stories like skin all the while and
not regretting it in the slightest, all set to the jive-talking jazz-jumping
boosted-bass-bumping boogie woogie rumble of a dream—

tympamania

Somebody once told me home is where the heart is
but what, exactly,
is a heart?

Is it something dark and beating
way down in Africa
(where I left my tongue and my skin
and my eyes and my pride)?
or maybe it's a thing
–red and bleeding–
in an insipid little town in Texas
or maybe
it's a lump of meat under my ribcage,
pumping blood through my aortas

and this has all gone on for too long

coda

here's a coda for you:
I learned to lie from my father
and just like him
I'm bad at it.

when I was born they told me the meaning of life
but
I forgot
(my bad)

Ugh.
I should've crawled back in

II.

AN ELEGY FOR THE STILL LIVING

el·e·gy
noun
a poem of serious reflection, typically a lament for the dead.

Last night's still swimming around in my belly:
embers of tequila are bouncing in the ether,
coiled snug like a snake around the inside of my skull

(oh mama, pity me,
I done drank too much)

but while I was laughing and
pissing and crying
and trying to sing
I remembered all the things
I forgot when I was born

and I put them down right here

sorry about that

because I knew right then, indelibly,
that everything in the whole world is either

    A.) dead
      or
    B.) dying

so this must be an elegy – a poem of mourning –
for all the dead who are still living

some friendly words of advice for the groom

Everything in you longs for the earth. You're built of mud, just like Adam, and just like Adam, you'll blame the whole thing on your wife.

order mammalia

I think sometimes
about our little family,
those who are like us,
the sensible creatures —
and by that I mean
those creatures which have senses
(and spines,
and six-layer frontal cortexes)

You know,
the higher species,
the beasts with hair:
the carnivores and the marsupials,
the ungulates and the rodentiforms.
Pigs and tigers, meerkats and manatees,
whales and dogs and camels
and apes,
the whole family,

the womb-born,
red-blooded
races;
that meat
which
of its own volition,
moves.

I think about them,
sometimes,
the mammals,

those sensible
creatures
who also give milk to
their young,
and all the many things we share.

For example:
the spine sense
that raises your hair,
the vicious heart
and the loosened bowel,
and all the many ways
that you *know*
when death
is near.

or that constant wish we all
share,

the wish either to
continue or to *be*
continued, the need
in your veins for a litter or a pup or
a brood

or even a darling little
nest —

because we cannot
forget the vampire bats,
who drink milk before blood,
who fling their young
from glittering cave walls,

who are also
part of the family.

and we all of us
know
like an old friend
that first and last need,
the piston drive
of all the higher orders:

hunger,
which is shared
by the seals
in the black
under the ice,
silver hunters
so far from the sun,
and the lioness, with
her jaws
so red,
who kills
for many other mouths,
and the stallion bent
so low
to pull the grass,
and by you,

just now,
sitting down for breakfast.

Yes
I think about them, sometimes.
The womb-born, red-blooded
races:
the family.

the odds

the odds were stacked against you from the start
so don't feel too bad:
they were stacked against us all

the wild radishes
sprouting
violent
among the weeds

the fish
circling blind in their tank

a woman
searching hopeless for
a word
she *used* to know

the rough
spiked
tongue of a tiger

a person
tall and upright by the side of the road as you pass them in your car,
who makes eye contact for just an instant and then is gone forever

banana groves
and schoolteachers

and schoolteachers in banana groves, and
fruit flies at noon,
black specks against the
sun

the true believers
and the scumbags

the egg
and the chicken
and the man with the chicken stunner

the it girls
who are not it anymore
and the boys who
very unfortunately
became men

the dogs,
stuck in
the rat race

the skinless
cities

full of people
spinning their wheels
with nowhere left to go

the spring flowers with
their mouths wide
open

for a rain that never comes

the
mocking birds

and the
straw eaters

the last living holdout
at the end of the line

and the many dead
who are still living
knee deep in the shit show

the odds
were stacked against them all

so don't feel too bad
if they were stacked
against you too

dancing

Me personally, I always thought that dancing was about the way
that fishnets catch turtles too, and cut their fluttering flippers with
razor wire like a chef cuts delicately into a steak to make sure it is no
longer bleeding. But I also always thought it was remarkably similar
to the numberless seconds one might spend watching their life slip
away, or the secret envy parents have for their children, which is
itself just a mirror of the cathartic violence against their parents
which all children wear naked on their sleeves and learn to hide
only when they are old and have children of their own, and it is also
about the time between the world wars when everyone was drunk
and glib and very lost and so they wrote poetry and killed themselves
because they could feel in their bones that there was another one
coming isn't that funny and it's also about the ways you layer on top
of yourself like sediment, a geological process of unspeakably slow
and shifting things in the inland parts of the soul, things which are
grinding glistening like the glaciers that slid across Pangaea, and
like the glaciers as they move forever changing everything caught
beneath their bulk, grinding away the whole world and leaving
behind permanent scars, and yet like the glaciers always moving
forward inexorably, and so like the glaciers melting slowly and
surely in the world they have made, which is why knowing another
person is like digging with raw hands through the earth's crust,
recording each layer of rock as you dig down, seeing with your own
eyes where the glaciers have passed and recording the shapes of the
pieces which they have carved off of themselves until you are too sad
or bored to go on, which is a bit like how moths see on all levels of
the electromagnetic spectrum, even in those ultraviolet wavelengths

which are invisible to the human eye, which is of course the reason why they are drawn in by electric lights, because to them they are a beauty greater than anything in nature which is not the sun, and that means both that some beauty, even for insects, must be worth dying for and also that nature is very cruel.

All of that is like dancing, when you get down to it. Dancing is also (of course) about sex — but they say everything is about sex.

spectacular

I dreamt a sort of dream
about things without a name
I saw a billion rats pacing the halls of a gilded maze,
and their fingers dug gouts in the gold as they went

all my days knotted together,
forming a plaque on the skin of my life;
a gingivitis, a biochemical gunk –
perhaps these many ways were not the ways we were meant to live

something faceless but familiar shifts off me like shed skin,
and I wonder, without irony, when I grew so old
I saw a shape so large it hurt to look at —
an idea so great it hurt to think —
a feeling so lonely it might have killed me had I felt it.
then I turned in my sleep, and shook it all away

the men of glass

my father took me aside
one dry november morning.
underneath a frigid and iron sky
he taught me all the paranoias of the working girl,
which of course are just justified belief.

these are a few of the things we talked about:
the blade glass, the tax code,
the price of the dollar in freefall,
and the cities all ablaze
like little matches in the night.

last of all he told me
of all those days yet to come:
the days of sweat and light.

'my girl',
he said to me, 'my beautiful baby girl,
those will be the days of the men of glass,
the ones you can see right through.'

well, he went on,
 these will, no doubt, be the
days of the body and rope
— the paint and the power —
the flesh and the form.

these will be,
if they are nothing else,
the days of the sun
and all her shapes
(hotter yet and hotter still).

but make no mistake,
he went on to say,
these will be above all
the days of the body,
red and raw,
more important than ever.

then my father described for me,
in as few words as he could,
how one may tell apart the men of glass:
the way they move – stiffly,
at the joints. their stilted speech,
which will never match their
breathing.

most importantly,
he said,
they will vibrate to a rhythm
which sets your teeth on edge,
a frequency
which may be seen
with the naked eye.

and you know, you feel it too,
what he felt.

even
if you are blind
or deaf,
you may catch it running
under the soles of your feet
like a live current, or

humming as it passes
between the sides of
your skull
and between the moving
pictures

between the hands
of the clock
between the cities
and the shore

between these moments
and their measure
between these
men
and their pleasure,
between the bodies
red and raw

between these many millions
with their noses to the sky

between the drifting continents,
faster than the waves.
listen:

feel it,
live it,
a buzzing,
a droning
right behind your teeth.

you know now
as I know
as my father knew, and
as every working girl
knows too:

these are the days of the men of glass
the ones
you can see
right through.

ten thousand things

The Chinese philosopher Lao Tzu says in his Tao Te Ching that heaven and earth and the ten thousand things are born of being,

and that being is born of nothing.

I'm not a philosopher, but I think about that all the time.

Here is what I think he meant.

You have gas station clerks and mountain climbers, you have salamanders and solar flares, you have unrepentant murderers and badly made chicken coops, you have tears smoking in the snow and you have the stinking sweat and heat of a million human bodies pressed together like sardines in a can, moving like liquid, you have the feeling of watching the unrehearsed ballet of a school of fish scattering before a predator (which is not very different from the beauty of first love or the shape of a collarbone under your thumb), you have a chorus of dogs barking minutes before midnight and keeping the whole world awake, you have an awkward but kind moment shared between two strangers on the street who do not speak the same language, you have a half-grown elephant cub peering curiously and stupidly down the barrel of a gun, you have cigarette butts floating on still water, you have the evils we do to ourselves and to each other —

these must be the ten thousand things.

but you also have a crooked stop sign so old that the S has faded and all it reads is TOP, and you have the distant silhouettes of mountains at midnight, and you have that insistent tugging feeling on your skin and your eyes and your very being that when you get old enough you realize is time itself, you have the ancient and unmoving bulk of the Ganges River, which was here before us and will be here after we're gone, you have the curious similarities between hunger and shit and gold, you have the mathematical and fractal perfection of haikus, you have the splendid shape of the continent called Africa and you have the decaying shells of old whaling factories off the coast of Newfoundland which have known countless red butcheries and now at night are used as nests for crabs, you have the rising oceans of the always-tomorrow and the winking glare of city lights on a black night and the quiet howling hum of a heater on a cold morning before a single soul has risen from sleep, you have the terrifying cage of the sky and the yawning eternity of the ground beneath our feet —

this must be earth.

and then you also have the feeling you get under your bones when you are alone and the world is quiet, you have good memories played over and over until they begin to wear out at the edges (just so, like a record), you have a righteous anger at the whole world and everything in it because it should be just a little bit better, you have the bitter aftertaste in an addicts' mouth which always chases the pleasure, you have the reason babies cry so loud when they look into a mirror, you have the deep dark thing way down inside that separates us from the other apes, you have the understanding that one day you'll die and the spark within you which refuses to accept it, you have all those big thoughts in your big brain which defy understanding and reason and time and space, you have the nauseating and indigestible feeling of being wholly perceived and understood by another thinking creature, you have the slow and heavy patterns which make up the rhythm of life, you have the quiet whistling deep inside your belly on an aimless night when the world refuses to fit together, you have the feeling that there *must* be an order to it all —

these, of course, are heaven.

Spake the Old Master: you have heaven and earth and the ten thousand things. They are born of being,

and being is born of nothing.

anthropocene

press your face into the dirt
and listen to the planet shake
after a long red while
you might hear,
from a long way away
the bones of your ancestors
getting it on
grinding themselves together,
grating one another to dust in the dark.

what?

people still have urges,
even the dead,
especially
the dead –
what else have they got to do?

they're going to be singing all the while,
keeping their graveyard tempo
with a little earworm of a tune;
belting out a little gospel,
red in truth and claw.

It's everything they wish
they'd done or been

or known before, and
it goes like this:

live on your feet
and do not be afraid

they do things differently in my country

In my country
there are ghosts staring from every street corner,
and the subway whistle comes loud like Gabriel's horn,
and sons are little more than the long shadows of their fathers.

In my country
we have killed all the birds,
and the cities stand apart like strangers without trust,
and every living thing is so alone in its skin.

In my country
all the girls have long legs
and carry razors loosely wrapped in the tangles of their hair.

In my country
the smell of new rain
lives on for many years in the dirt.

In my country all the old women know the secret of life,
but they only share it written on the bathroom stalls in lipstick,
where the men can't see.

In my country children climb the telephone poles
not to get a better view,
but to let their better angels dangle in the wind.

In my country
the street stones mumble their histories in the dead of night
and the buildings stare stupidly with all love lost as you pass them by

In my country
we pay homage to the still living.

In my country
we are trying to remember how to apologize.

In my country
we wear our sins like shirts of knife wire.

In my country
we are pilgrims not yet born.
In my country
there are a thousand and one things yet to be.

In my country we are aware of ourselves
as being just and only animals

in my country
in my country
in my country
in my country
the sun eats you as you face it.

in-between people

Some folks
do not live like everybody else.
They are mad folks, bad folks,
rotten-to-the-bone folks,
never-held-a-9-to-five-folks,
people of the bottle,
folks who smoke too much
and have too little,
who turn tricks and key cars,
whom nobody likes and who like nobody in return,
who have lots of love to give and give it
to just about anyone,
who live right here one day and out there the next,
who tattooed themselves one night high out of their minds,
using just ink and a pen and a vision,
and found it didn't look half bad anyway,
who once in their twenties left somewhere they called home
and never looked back,
who would sooner steal a dollar than ask for one,
because of something more stubborn than pride,
really, it's not like pride at all, it is
something hard and rigid and fundamentally human at the base of
their spine,
but still
stupid anyway.
Those folks,
the ratty overgrown teenagers,
the beat-up single mothers,

the entitled couch surfers and
the selfish subway tokers,
those children of the sun and
those daughters of the night
those walkers with cats and
babies whose parents
regretted it —
the ones who are too violent,
and the many more who are not violent enough,
those folks,
who are more jealous than you can imagine
but regret less than you might think,
who laugh at everything and have skin like seals —
because everything, and I mean anything,
just slides right off.

I think about them often:
those folks
who
do not live like everybody else,
who were a long time coming
and will be a long time going,
who are the raw body of the whole human race.

on waking up on saturday

sometimes you wake up on saturday
with a mouth full of constellations
wet and bloody on your tongue,
and with them are the ten thousand things
pulled from the ten thousand nights
and sharpened like
the lead of a pencil
to the very point
of your
flesh.

and when this knowledge goes,
you are left with some unmistakable sensation
that your spinal cord is moving in *coils*, in rings,
like a beast that shivers when it is not cold,

and that way
in the back of your
throat

there is an animal's
voice.

the trick of all flesh

wait until time seems to drop back on itself like a wave, then feel the
various ways that life itself stretches out: like a balloon swelling too
fast, or an oar swinging wide, or a tree struck by lightning standing
violently still while the world rolls away. On the side of a highway
in the southern parts of every country you can care to name there
are red flowers blooming stubborn in the winter, the edges of their
petals sharp and red and cracked with frost. They do not understand
that they should be dead, and so they are alive. A golden crust
wrapped thin about fresh bread, flaky yet tender, and still warm
from the oven. Wind moving on a lake dark as wine, stirring black
waves on the water. The flickering light inside the skull of a bird.
The implacable hunger of the grass right before the rain falls, and
the swelling fullness after it has. The tidal rhythms of the blood
moving tight under your skin. The concrete veins of a city laid out
in cold and shining grids. The many hells of earth. A hatred which
jerks through your heart like the flat edge of a blade. That feeling of
time rolling over like an iron wheel, and the feeling that follows the
feeling, which you have always had but never admitted: that between
the spokes of that iron wheel there is a sharp and silent wind,
blowing hard, a wind which is gunmetal cold and cuts like glass.

you seek, invariably, impotently, a way to hide your skin from that
razor wind.

there is no way, not that I know,
but there *is* a trick,
tried and true
and this is the trick of all flesh:

swallow your
own throat: try
to eat your name.
if you must kiss,
kiss deeper than skin.
forgive badly:
hold few grudges
but hold them well.

do not,
under any circumstances,
pay your debts.

you will lie anyway,
so lie often,
or you will not know how to
when you need to.

most importantly,
you should cry easily, like a child,
or not at all.

and remember:
there is no
new thing
under
the sun

thank god.

delphi

He wishes to love like the swingers love,
without reservation, or guilt, or shame,
with nothing on his back
and nothing to his name.

But he's too young to understand how,
and too old to try again.

She tells others their fortunes,
here in this place.

She sees nothing at all,
— no eyes in that face —
but she is not blind:

She wrings herself out,
tight like a dishrag,
and reads little futures
in the shapes left behind.

He asks her for love,
or for love's smallest secret,
or for one, perhaps, of love's many names.

But the god —love's own brother—
who speaks through her mouth,
who has wrung out all her days,

who spells out the future in the shapes
left behind —

the god
is not kind.

elegy for the still living

and our culture is skinless, you understand:
it is bristling all over with these hollow things,
these mosquito cities, swollen
almost to bursting,
yet still drinking deep of human fat

it is tongueless, toothless, mouthless, blind,
a closed book,
a division of zero,
a mirror mirroring nothing

      going nowhere
      thinking nothing worth thinking,
a corpse culture, plastic, cold,
      an engine burning without fuel,
a thing itself alone,
for itself alone

but crawling like lice upon the corpse
are people
not hollow yet, not toothless yet, not tongueless yet, not mouthless
yet,
and not blind
yet

flow lightning, ii

Do you want to feel the music
which links skins to skins?
You know: the slow music,
the kissing thing,
that jazzy bounce in the limbic zone –
the heart stuff and the flow stuff –
the mind stuff, the know stuff.

whatever it is inside of us
that looks at a
child's hand and sees infinite glories,
and the promise of too many things
too far beyond,
the promise that we are just this,
and more than this,
that we are this alone,
and everything else besides —

that thing.

flick the switch
or pull the trigger
or turn the key.
let the lights crackle on,
wait as the AC hums vibrato
and the engines kick into high gear.

you feel it
snap *through* you
right then,
the lightning.

just for a second,
as it all flares to life,
you can taste it
moving on your tongue.

the things that the living know

here are the things that the living know:

legs about to crack from the strain of holding up your body, tendons
white at the bone, lungs stretching to the edge, pressure building
inside like a cooker bomb, a gaping and widening length between
the fibers of your muscles, cold spirals of dark brass felt underneath
your hand but never seen, thin black roofs bellowing like Irish
drums under the weight of too much rain, slug sick prophet things
crawling up out of the gullets of the poets, the halting shadow of
someone else's hand in the dark, the sly knowing of cats moving
lightly like a mirror on the skin, paper boats suspended on slow
rivers, small islands disappeared in the shadows of continents, the
desire to simply sit and rot it out and the sister compulsion to fit
inside your mouth everything you do not have room to be, skin and
bone and something more cracking at the joints, men joining rough
hands at the very end, the mad urge of an age which is too slick like
wet rock, lurching flames seen in the distance across dark water, the
midday noon warm and familiar on your back in the streets of San
Juan, the low and easy purr of a trumpet like something ancient
from the throat of a tiger, the crack and the boom, the shake and the
roar, the knife and the narrow, and all around you in the tightness of
your pores the very stink of life

the absolute reek of it

those are the things the living know.

cascade

I don't have the answers
I don't know the way
I very much maybe might not know anything at all
but I do know this:

A million droplets make a wave:

one on top another,
repeating and repeating

until they all
cascade

III.

METAPHYSICS OF THE EGO

met·a·phys·ics
noun
the branch of philosophy that deals with the first principles of
things, including abstract concepts such as being, knowing,
substance, cause, identity, time, and space.

Imagine a jungle of obsidian pyramids, over which reigns a titanic black sphinx with ivory eyes like cold white oceans. He is scrawling with a stone pen in a massive book with black stone pages, and each letter he writes is punctuated by the grinding of stone on stone. The words he is writing are the words in my head.

Beyond him, nightmare edifices give way to a vast and endless forest of elder trees coated in winter white, pale and cold and still as bones. The snow is unbroken. Monolithic black engines churn noiselessly in the distance, rising and falling to some inexorable and terrible purpose. Between the leaves and the eaves, men in black robes toil at profane rituals under tall altars, and all the while they are grinning toothless grins. As they labor at their task, they are raising their voices to a pitiful groaning song. The words they are singing are the words in my head.

This, too, gives way to black towers and black streets in a black city, black on black on black, slate on pitch on shadow, and every surface in the city is a mirror into night. Every building is studded with black stone steps which echo loudly with the drumming footsteps of a million hooded figures, every one of whom is marching in a slow and silent funeral dirge, gliding up and down countless rows of stairs in endless melancholy. Each of these million figures is wearing a mask, and each of those million masks is as white as pearl. There are words carved on the many steps they walk and the many masks they wear, and those many words are the words in my head.

And these are the words in my head:

THE ME THE MORE THE ME THE MORE THE ME
THE MORE THE ME THE MORE THE ME THE
MORE THE ME THE MORE THE ME THE MORE
THE ME

TRANSMUTATION

something lived naked under her skin
growing always, growing ever
growing stronger –
it slid out one bright Sunday morning
PUSHING PULLING RIPPING RISING
soaked in gore and sex and sin
and all else that is fine under the sun
annihilation is the name of the game
one way or another
bite your gut and chew the shame
rinse your eyes with bleach and blink
can you see it yet?
somewhere black engines are turning
under psychotropic skies
pulsing curving shaking burning
like a mother on the birthing bed
and each and every one swells with tears –
why?
and I wake somewhere else I cannot name
on the far side of the sun
(a different sort of light shines there:
it is DIM and DRY)

and that mammoth sphinx
with coal for skin
sits
and writes with a stone pen
scritching scratching scratching scritching
in the book with stone pages
and the words it writes
are the words in my head

her face is a window
outside is eternity
I hang on a tightrope
between dissolution
and disaster

she is the backbeat
the heartbeat
the super-sweet
(of poison or candy,
I can't tell)

her lips
boiled
and steamed
I stripped the paper from them
and drank what lay beneath
but it was not sweet at all

it was sour and it soured me

or perhaps I was sick already

the she-wolf, the lupus whore
in her jaws
is everything
the need, the want, the me, the more
the window is stained glass
and there are no saints

my bones walk when I dream
my mother guides them
as I roam
up tight black streets packed thick with icy souls
through cities like glass mazes
and years like steel cages
past men with white faces
before I was the I that I am
I was another I
and the I that I was
waded up fresh from the island foam
that will always be my home
(though I did not choose it)

there an *I* will always be:
in bright lurid jungles
in older darker days
keeping time as I run
to the tantric beating of the sun
and the frantic pounding of the sea
as I run forever on
with those who hid
and were free

nah jah
why did you forsake us?
ELOI, ELOI,
we were your children, too

there is a pattern to all of this
the mythos repeats
the archetypes are static

this world is a story
and every climax is its climax
every *petit-mort* its denouement
they wrap the world in rags
and put out the sun's eyes
so she cannot see
what they are doing to her children

LUPERCALIA

I saw the thing that lived under her skin;
it is a tale told nowhere else
and lives now only IN ME:
it is black and shaggy all over
and fanged and rude and proud
with eyes like cold marbles
and teeth like butcher's knives,
flensing innocence
swallowing lives
(my memories may be biased)
(I was very scared at the time)
but
above all
I know this:
it hungers

a symphony, in eight parts:
sound and fury
flesh and fire
Myself and I
and the Conqueror Worm
(so PROUD is he)
and of course
the all-mastering,
the all-devouring
the all-conquering
SHE

this signifies nothing!
and yet, right now,
it is everything

     can you feel the
     blood-pulse,
     the life-rhythm,
     the bone-drumming,

     the insistence
     of existence
going round and round your skull in circles?

this is it
this is all there is and all that is you:
the back-beat and the heart-beat,
the dull aching endless roar
of your thoughts
in your head;

     learned very well, but
     THIS ALONE IS TRUE:

no man made this

no hand shaped it

nothing made me but myself*

nothing but me (and her, of course)**

nothing but me and the dark men in their dark jungles in their dark days, who had the children who made the children that made the children who were the slaves that were freed and had the children that had the children that had me

*and the faces of my father

**and the beast that was in her

I look and see seven times seven
I am historical and numerical, superfluous and superlative
CAN YOU SEE THE PATTERN SHINE?
spake both the angel and the ape
I AM BUT A THING DIVINE:
A MISTAKE

lurching slurching slurping searching
I have had enough of lies
do what I did
crack your father's skull
see the world through his eyes

interlude: sepsis

sep-sis:
a divorce
of the relations between
a body and it's constituent parts
— say, the blood, or the heart,
or the lungs.

the immune system no longer
recognizes them
as part of itself.

the familiar becomes understood
as foreign, is attacked
as a stranger,
and is quickly
killed.

suppose
that god is a thing with ears?

spaces and voices and places
and rows
of golden horses champing at the bit
below a sky like a bell dome carved
all of glass (under which rise
temples of the sun
black tipped like felt markers).

suppose that god
is a thing with ears?

I can see it, sometimes:
how the certain lines
will deepen, as river valleys.
one day I will have smiled
too much and then I'll be old.

a whole city
might live and die in that sentence.

suppose, even then,
that god is a thing with ears?

last week, I went in for a job interview.
The guy was white, but on the wall
above his desk, there was an image,
carved in wood, of the Mexican general Santa Anna —
who was president of Mexico seven times and lost Texas to the
United States,
who was the most vulgar of the caudillos,
who was the Phyrrus of the New World,
who was a failed man of destiny, who failed his people and himself,
and who later introduced chewing gum
to the USA.

I took it for the ill omen
which it was, and I left.
do you suppose that god
is a thing with ears?

the future moves towards me,
a wheel or a wave rising.

it's warm under my collar, and
I find that the many parts of my body
are growing lighter and lighter,
as if they may soon
no longer wish to
hold themselves
together.

everywhere, I am hemmed in
by little obligations
like barbed wire, and
sometimes, to put more of Earth
under my feet, I look into a mirror
and I plot out the geography of
my father's face. do you suppose
that god is a thing with ears?

but today, I am young and warm
and everybody has been born,
and everybody is dying,
and there is the wind like an enemy
and there are women in the world
squatting to give birth over a grave.

I am becoming very certain
that life is an accretion or an accumulation
of many different things, and that heaven
is a place right over there,
like Mexico.

WHAT IS THE MEASURE OF A MAN?
divide a suit by a life by a lie by a tale told by cracked and
bleeding lips and add equal cups of bitterness and kindness

multiply it all by the silence in your skull

and then add

the past,
(most likely a lie)
the future,
(looming dark ahead)
promising and threatening and destroying and liberating
(like the barrel of a gun to the head)
and last of all
the tyrant now

solve for the fact that we have builded our house upon oil and
blood
and ecstasy

and the rock is slick
so very slick
and the waves crashing all about are so very high
and *the eyes of all the dead are upon all the living*
you understand we're failing them?
(It's okay, they failed us)
what is the measure of man?

show him the slave and hand him the whip
and see him raise it high
he's done it before
he'll do it again

there's something inside her
I think it wants to EAT ME

...there's something inside me, too
(I think it wants to eat her)

seas thick with jet black ichor that makes the jets track
seeping into the soil and the soul and the silk and the sinners
into
slick scales and pitted shells,
a stomach packed thick until it swells
with kitchen liners and Saran Wrap,
and coke cans and cookie cutters
and the thousand and one knickknack poisons
all sleeping on the ocean floor,
rotting away a hair of a hair slower than forever,
choking everything that dares to live
and they are all throbbing in time
with the inescapable hum of the plastic
sitting cold in your wallet and your heart and your lungs
and your brain

the rock is slick

and there are hungry voiceless whines in the dark
children or animals?
does it matter?
should it?
will it?
has it?

I am
I was
I have been
I always will be
And yet I am unfilled and unfulfilled;
Something voiceless and hungry whines in the dark

stop

back it up

start from the top

The Kingdom, Animalia
The Phylum, Chordata
The Class, Mammalia
the genus, Homo (no relation)

well, you know the rest

all this and all that and a little bit more
(and quite a bit less);
that is the measure of a man

APOTHEOSIS

We echo back into ourselves, a ping-ponging sing-song
singalong made in pain by the vain

(but what more, a white-faced nun intones in a voice like

breaking chalk, what more could possibly be expected from the children of Cain?)

Here is my confession:

There is a beast in me too:
He has proud eyes
And teeth like knives
And a fat red tongue dripping lies
Once, I hated him, but now it's fine:
I understand he is a thing divine.

It makes no sense to try and make sense of nonsense, (especially since common sense is no sense at all), hence:

and WHEREFORE, and WHY,

The natural state of all existence is entropy, decay, and when you remember that it becomes really quite crystal clear that the act of living is an act of rebellion. If the natural state of the natural world is nothing then TO BE is an act against nature. Things are still or they move, and the universe trends slowly and coldly and surely toward stillness, toward an endless and empty day ten trillion years in the future when the last bit of kinetic energy left over from the Big Bang shudders to a stop and the stars freeze over and the skies fall silent and all across the infinite universe not one single solitary thing burns or breathes or moves or dreams.

In the face of such certainty all acts are rebellion, and life most of all.

I LOOKED (into the future)
and beheld a PALE HORSE
and the name of
  He
    that rode on it —
I did not hear, because I laughed in his face.

The universe will grow cold one day. The sum total of everything that was or will be is a cold zero. And so it seems silly that the stars still shine and the world still spins and that we argue about maps and batteries and the too-high price of gas. It seems that nobody and nothing should move at all, for the futility of it.

AND YET
IT MOVES

pulsing and beating like a liar's heart or
a wire-bound drum on a hot summer
afternoon in the bay when the waves are high

the entire wet glorious thriving whole of it
driving relentless and silly and ignorant,
and moving all the same – up, up! –
moving to the rhythm that is
pounding in the skull
of every tiger and every child,
every soldier and every dragonfly

this is the staccato refrain of the stuff in our brain:
do not stop do not breathe do not wait do not hesitate
keep going keep living keep beating keep pulsing
keep pounding
keep being

this is the back-beat behind your heart-beat:

THE MORE THE MORE THE MORE THE MORE THE MORE THE MORE THE ME
and when you look of out your window on at night and you see the headlights of strange cars passing by ghostlike in the darkness and you imagine for a single unbroken moment what each of those lives and their stories might be like, and you *feel* a thing which you have no name for, you should hold it tight:
that is the matter and the meat.

awake, arise, aspire — adhere
lust, want, desire — fear

she was not sour,
I just did not know how to drink

WHEN I COME BACK TO MYSELF

I am so far above and so far below

I am dreaming, and in dreams I of course have mothlike wings
of silver fire, which carry me over a black planet on the far side of
the sun (where the light is DIM and DRY), where silent pyramids sit
jungled in the darkness, and a stone sphinx with hideous eyes writes
ponderously in a book of heathen stone.

and the words it writes
are the words in my head,
and mine alone.

In my dream
I stand atop that mighty head and gaze into those lidless eyes
(white, like the sea-foam on an all-too-familiar shore)

and the words I hear then are the words in my head:
the me the me the me the me the me the me the more

About the Author

Kenan Phillip is a Dominica-born poet living along the Texas-Mexico border, where he is currently pursuing an MFA in Creative Writing at the University of Texas Rio Grande Valley. Currently, he serves as Volunteer Coordinator and board member of the Unfolded Poetry Project, a poetry-centered nonprofit based in the RGV. He is currently working on a creative thesis exploring intercultural and Afro-Caribbean/Latino poetics, decolonialism, and the poetics of relation.

FLOWERSONG
P R E S S

**FlowerSong Press nurtures essential verse
from, about, and throughout the borderlands.
Literary. Lyrical. Boundless.**

Sign up for announcements about
new and upcoming titles at:

www.flowersongpress.com